Little Lost Kitten

by Caroline Hoile
Edited by Alison Hedger

A fanciful story for Christmas time with seven songs.
A full performance will include music, mime, movement,
and dance. Speaking parts may be given as appropriate.

Duration approx. 25 mins.

For children 4 to 7 years Key Stage 1
Also suitable for Pre- School Groups and Special Education Units.

TEACHER'S BOOK
The story, songwords, music and production notes included.

SONGS

1. Christmas!
2. Oh Where Are You? *This song recurs as the search takes place throughout the story.*
3. Squeaky, Jumping Mice
4. Miaow, Miaow
5. Spiky, Spiny Hedgehogs
6. Quack, Quack
7. We've Found You At Last

A matching tape cassette of the music for rehearsals and performances is available,
Order No. GA 10925 side A with vocals included, side B with vocals omitted.

© Copyright 1994 Golden Apple Productions
A division of Chester Music Limited
8/9 Frith Street, London W1V 5TZ

Order No. GA10913 ISBN 0-7119-4162-9

"I hope everyone will have fun with this mini-musical, which provides a fanciful story for Christmas time. The LITTLE LOST KITTEN is not a Nativity and is meant to be enjoyed by children of all faiths. The closing reference to the Christian side of Christmas is deliberate, but can be omitted if required. I am aware that cats do not have "feet" and that hedgehogs hibernate!!

Best wishes to you all."

Caroline Hoile

PRODUCTION NOTES

The following notes are kept as brief as possible. Teachers and children, will have their own ideas. The LITTLE LOST KITTEN can be done as simply as possible with the minimum of staging and costume and so can be enjoyed in a class situation. Alternatively, the musical can be staged with props, costumes, miming and choreographed dance sequences, making a most enjoyable school production to share with families and friends.

CHARACTERS

> Mabel the Mother Cat
> Four Kittens
> * Mice
> * Alley Cats
> * Hedgehogs
> * Ducks
> * Snowmen

*These groups can include as many participants as necessary.

SPEAKING PARTS

The story can be read by a member of staff, or perhaps some older children might read parts of the narrative from flash cards.

Speaking parts can be "lifted" from the story. eg Mabel's dialogue. Individual children or groups can say "We haven't seen her. But we'll certainly look out for her now." etc. This obviously depends on individual circumstances.

SCENES

The story subdivides into 6 "scenes", making the LITTLE LOST KITTEN an ideal work for several classes to come together in a joint production. Each class is allocated a scene. The marking ✹ in the script denotes each "scene" change.

ACTIONS

These are suggested by the narrative and song words. Either let the children spontaneously act out their ideas, or make a more formal presentation by "choreographing" sequences. Either way, it will be fun!

SCENERY

This is not necessary, but if subdividing the work into "scenes", each group could paint its own backdrop. eg garden, park etc. Remember the action takes place in the snow, after dark. The lighting colours are indicated for the most part, in the narrative; eg the street lamps cast an orange glow.

COSTUMES

Great ingenuity will come to bear on the hedgehog costumes. Other characters are dressed as would be expected in a production for this age range. Making and wearing a costume is all part of the fun, however amateurish the final results might be!

PROPS

As many and as elaborate as desired.

THE SONGS

The songs have been written to appeal to young children. The piano accompaniments are simple yet effective. Chord symbols are included for those wishing to use an electronic keyboard or guitar. Please add in percussion and sound effects to colour the music if you feel it worthwhile in your particular circumstances. Repeat any/all of the songs as many times as required for the dances.

LITTLE LOST KITTEN

It was Christmas Eve. The moon shone brightly in the darkening sky. The frosty air was cold and still. A sprinkling of snow lay on the ground and all the earth was frozen hard.

But inside the house where Mabel the cat lived with her four fluffy kittens, it was quite different. A friendly fire crackled in the grate and gave the room a rosy glow. The mantelpiece was bedecked with joyful Christmas cards and colourful streamers twisted and twirled in every place that could be imagined. An elegant fir tree stood gracefully by the window, dancing with shiny baubles and looking most beautiful. The whole house smelt deliciously with the promise of gorgeous food. And, of course, the stockings had been hung up with excitement, in the hope that Father Christmas would soon fill them with presents.

Mabel the cat and her four fluffy kittens stretched out in the cosy warmth and rolled around playfully. They agreed that it really was all quite perfect!

SONG 1   **CHRISTMAS!**

Chorus   It's frosty, it's icy, it's cold as can be,
The snowflakes have fallen, it's winter you see!
It's frosty, it's icy, it's cold as can be,
But it's Christmas time and it's precious to me.

Verse   Christmas brings happiness,
Christmas brings joyfulness,
Christmas brings hope to everyone.
You can share our happiness,
You can share our joyfulness,
And have a perfect time.

Chorus   It's frosty... etc.

But it didn't stay perfect for long. All of a sudden, things changed! The front door opened, just for a second, and in the twinkling of an eye, one little ginger kitten, with a stripy tail, dashed outside and scampered away, out into the cold dark night. She did not come back.

Mabel the cat leapt to the door and looked outside. The little kitten was nowhere to be seen. Mabel miaowed a hurried "goodbye" to her other fluffy kittens and rushed out into the bitter coldness of the night, to look for the little lost ginger kitten with the stripy tail.

SONG 2   **OH WHERE ARE YOU?**

Oh where are you?
Oh where are you?
Pussycat where have you gone?
Oh where are you?
Oh where are you?
Please don't be long!

Mabel the cat squeezed through a hole in the wooden gate and found herself in the back garden. The moon shimmered high in the sky and cast silver beams over the icy landscape.

Mabel searched everywhere. She looked behind clumps of frozen flowers that stood straight and stiff. She looked into flowerpots that had tumbled over. She looked in the wheelbarrow that was half filled with snow. But she couldn't see the little lost kitten anywhere.

Mabel was just about to leave the garden when she suddenly heard a rustling sound coming from the garden shed. She pricked up her ears, miaowed gently and rushed over to the shed. But instead of seeing her little lost kitten, she found herself staring at a huge family of squeaky mice.

SONG 3   SQUEAKY, JUMPING MICE

1.   Lots and lots of little mice, squeaking everywhere we go.
     Lots and lots of little mice, squeaking high and squeaking low.
         Squeak up here! Squeak down there!
         Somewhere in the middle! Now guess where!
     Lots and lots of little mice, squeaking everywhere we go.

2.   Lots and lots of little mice, jumping everywhere we go.
     Lots and lots of little mice, jumping high and jumping low.
         Jump up here! Jump down there!
         Somewhere in the middle! Now guess where!
     Lots and lots of little mice, jumping everywhere we go.

Repeat verse 1

1.   Lots and lots of little mice, squeaking... etc.

Mabel purred with disappointment. "Excuse me, little mice," miaowed Mabel the cat. "My little ginger kitten with a stripy tail is lost. Have you seen her anywhere?"

The mice looked up high and they looked down low. They looked to the right and they looked to the left. But they couldn't see the little lost kitten anywhere. The huge family of squeaky mice shook their heads sadly and tweaked their tails. "No," they squeaked. "We haven't seen her. But we'll certainly look out for her now."

(REPEAT) SONG 2   OH WHERE ARE YOU?

Oh where are you?
Oh where are you?
Pussycat where have you gone?
Oh where are you?
Oh where are you?
Please don't be long!

Mabel the cat went out into the street. The street lamps lit up the black night with a warm orange glow, which bathed the frozen, slippery pavements in pools of light.

Mabel the cat searched everywhere. She looked under cars that were silently parked on the road. She looked into the red post box, now emptied of all its Christmas cards. She looked around the telephone box standing hushed and still. But she couldn't see the little lost kitten anywhere.

Mabel was just about to leave the street when she suddenly heard a rustling sound coming from the nearby dustbins. She pricked up her ears, miaowed gladly and rushed over to the dustbins. But instead of seeing her little lost kitten, she found herself peering at a whole streetful of howling alley cats.

SONG 4 **MIAOW, MIAOW**

1. Prowling around in the alley,
Prowling on velvety feet.
Prowling around in the alley,
You never know who you will meet!
Miaow, miaow,
Miaow, miaow.
You never know who you will meet!

2. Howling around in the alley,
Howling so shrill in the street.
Howling around in the alley,
You never know who you will meet!
Miaow, miaow,
Miaow, miaow.
You never know who you will meet!

Mabel purred with disappointment. "Excuse me, prowling alley cats," miaowed Mabel the cat. "My little ginger kitten with a stripy tail is lost. Have you seen her anywhere?"

The alley cats looked up high and they looked down low. They looked to the right and they looked to the left. But they couldn't see the little lost kitten anywhere. The whole streetful of howling alley cats shook their heads sadly and curled their whiskers " No," they howled, "we haven't seen her. But we'll certainly look out for her now."

(REPEAT) SONG 2   OH WHERE ARE YOU?

Oh where are you?
Oh where are you?
Pussycat where have you gone?
Oh where are you?
Oh where are you?
Please don't be long!

Mabel the cat climbed carefully down to the nearby railway station. Jack Frost had touched the now deserted railway tracks, making them glitter, sparkly and bright.

Mabel the cat searched everywhere. She looked under the railway bridge, which was covered in spiky icicles. She miaowed into the dark tunnel, which echoed hollowly back. She looked under the seats on the silent, cold platform. But she couldn't see the little lost kitten anywhere.

Mabel was just about to leave the station when she heard a rustling sound coming from the railway embankment. She pricked up her ears, miaowed gladly and rushed over to the embankment. But instead of seeing her little lost kitten she found herself peering at an enormous gang of snuffling hedgehogs.

SONG 5   **SPIKY, SPINY HEDGEHOGS**

1.   Spiky, spiny hedgehogs are we.
Slugs and snails we eat for our tea.
   If you come too close to us,
   We curl up very small!
Spiky, spiny hedgehogs are we.
Slugs and snails we eat for our tea.

2.   Spiky, spiny hedgehogs are we.
Slugs and snails we eat for our tea.
   When it's very cold outside,
   We curl up very small!
Spiky, spiny hedgehogs are we.
Slugs and snails we eat for our tea.

3.   Spiky, spiny hedgehogs are we.
Slugs and snails we eat for our tea.
   When we're tired we go to sleep,
   We curl up very small!
Spiky, spiny hedgehogs are we.
Slugs and snails we eat for our tea.

Mabel purred with disappointment. "Excuse me, prickly hedgehogs," miaowed Mabel the cat. "My little ginger kitten with a stripy tail is missing. Have you seen her anywhere?"

The hedgehogs looked up high and they looked down low. They looked to the right and they looked to the left. But they couldn't see the little lost kitten anywhere. The enormous gang of snuffling hedgehogs shook their heads sadly and blinked their bright eyes. "No," they snuffled. "We haven't seen her, but we'll certainly look out for her now."

(REPEAT) SONG 2   OH WHERE ARE YOU?

Oh where are you?
Oh where are you?
Pussycat where have you gone?
Oh where are you?
Oh where are you?
Please don't be long!

Mabel the cat crept silently into the park. The bright stars twinkled in the sky and the light from the wintry moon cast peculiar shadows on the ground.

Mabel the cat searched everywhere. She looked up at the trees, standing tall and stark. She looked round the swings, now motionless and abandoned. She looked hard at the snowmen, who smiled smugly back. But she couldn't see the little lost kitten anywhere.

Mabel was just about to leave the park when she suddenly heard a rustling sound coming from the frozen pond. She pricked up her ears, miaowed gladly and rushed over to the pond. But instead of her little lost kitten she found herself peering at a giant huddle of quacking ducks.

SONG 6   **QUACK, QUACK**

1.   Quack, quack, quack, quack,
                 Quacking all day long.
             Quack, quack, quack, quack,
                 Listen to our song.
             Quack, quack, quack, quack,
                 Flying through the air.
             Quack, quack, quack, quack,
                 Flapping everywhere.

2.   Quack, quack, quack, quack,
                 Head tucked under wing.
             Quack, quack, quack, quack,
                 On one leg standing.
             Quack, quack, quack, quack,
                 Eating bits of bread.
             Quack, quack, quack, quack,
                 Dabbling beaks instead.

3.   Quack, quack, quack, quack,
                 Waddling all around.
             Quack, quack, quack, quack,
                 Slipping on the ground.
             Quack, quack, quack, quack,
                 Bottoms in the air.
             Quack, quack, quack, quack,
                 Do you have to stare?

Coda   Do you have to stare?

Mabel purred with disappointment. She sat down wearily by the side of the pond. She thought that she would never see her little lost kitten again and she sobbed pitifully.

The feathery ducks shook their heads sadly and flapped their wings. "Mabel the cat," they quacked. "Don't be so sad. We have a wonderful surprise for you." Then the giant huddle of quacking ducks jumped up high and they stretched down low. They shuffled to the right and they shuffled to the left. And out from the very centre of the huddle sprang the little lost kitten!

Mabel the cat miaowed with delight. The little ginger kitten with the stripy tail purred with pleasure. The fluffy ducks quacked with excitement and waddled a little dance. The little lost kitten had been found at last!

SONG 7   **WE'VE FOUND YOU AT LAST**

We've found you at last,
We've found you at last.
Pussycat where did you go?
We've found you at last,
We've found you at last.
We missed you so!

(Repeat the music as many times as necessary to perform a celebration dance with hand claps and skips. It may be a good idea to include not only Mabel, the kitten and the ducks, but also some mice, alley cats and hedgehogs.)

It was Christmas Day. The sun shone brightly in the clear blue sky. The frosty air was cold and still. A sprinkling of fresh snow lay on the ground and all the earth was frozen hard.

But inside the house where Mabel the cat lived with her four fluffy kittens, it was quite different. A friendly fire crackled in the grate and gave the room a rosy glow. The mantelpiece was bedecked with joyful Christmas cards and colourful streamers twisted and twirled in every place that could be imagined. An elegant fir tree stood gracefully by the window, dancing with shiny baubles and looking most beautiful. The whole house smelt deliciously with the promise of gorgeous food. And Father Christmas had filled the stockings right up to the brim with exciting presents. Church bells rang out to celebrate the special day and joyful singing announced the birth of the Baby King.

Mabel the cat and her four fluffy kittens stretched out in the cosy warmth and rolled around playfully. They agreed that it really was all quite perfect!

FINALE (REPEAT) SONG 1 CHRISTMAS!

Chorus

It's frosty, it's icy, it's cold as can be,
The snowflakes have fallen, it's winter you see!
It's frosty, it's icy, it's cold as can be,
But it's Christmas time and it's precious to me.

Verse

Christmas brings happiness,
Christmas brings joyfulness,
Christmas brings hope to everyone.
You can share our happiness,
You can share our joyfulness,
And have a perfect time.

Chorus

It's frosty… etc.

THE END

SONG 1
CHRISTMAS!

Cue both first time and for FINALE: They agreed that it really was all quite perfect.

SONG 1
CHRISTMAS!

Cue both first time and for FINALE: They agreed that it really was all quite perfect.

Happily ♩ = 96
(no chords)

Chorus

It's
It's

frost - y, ___ it's i - cy, ___ it's cold as can be, _____ the
frost - y, ___ it's i - cy, ___ it's cold as can be, ___ but it's

1st time   **2nd time**
B♭   E♭   F   B♭   B♭   **Fine**

snow - flakes have fal - len, ___ it's win - ter you see! ___   It's
Christ - mas ___ time and ___ it's pre - cious to me. ___

to finish

(turn page for song verse)

15

SONG 2
OH WHERE ARE YOU?

Cue: 1) …to look for the little ginger kitten with the stripy tail.

2), 3), and 4) But we'll certainly look out for her now.

SONG 3
SQUEAKY, JUMPING MICE

Cue: ... a huge family of squeaky mice.

Amy squeak

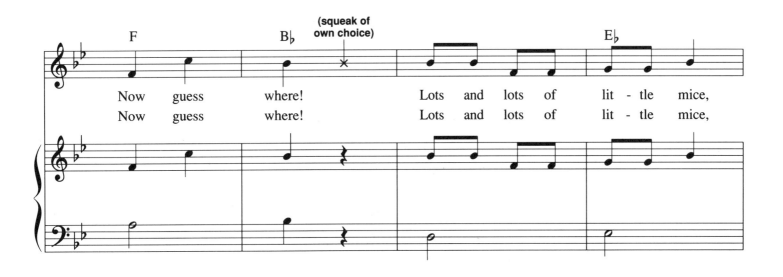

To conclude, repeat verse 1

SONG 4
MIAOW, MIAOW

Cue: … a whole streetful of howling alley cats.

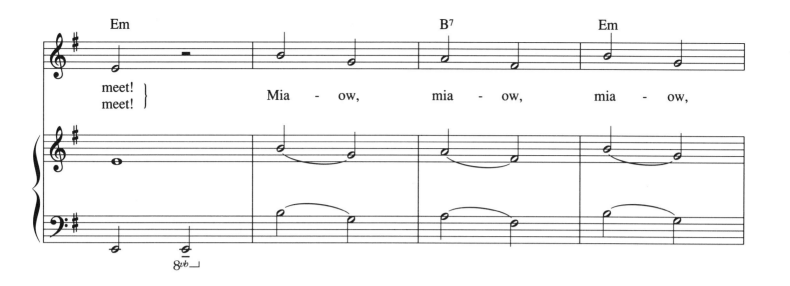

meet!
meet! } Mia - ow, mia - ow, mia - ow,

mia - ow.
{ You nev - er know who you___ will meet!
{ You nev - er know who you___ will meet!

MIAOW

SONG 5
SPIKY SPINY HEDGEHOGS

Cue: … at an enormous gang of snuffling hedgehogs.

Spi - ky, spi - ny hedge - hogs are we. _ Slugs and snails we

eat for our tea.

QUACK, QUACK

Cue: … a giant huddle of quacking ducks.

V1+2 quack flap

V3 - one leg
      standing on 1 leg

V4 - Hide now

V5 - Head down
      Bottoms in the air

V6 - Quack.

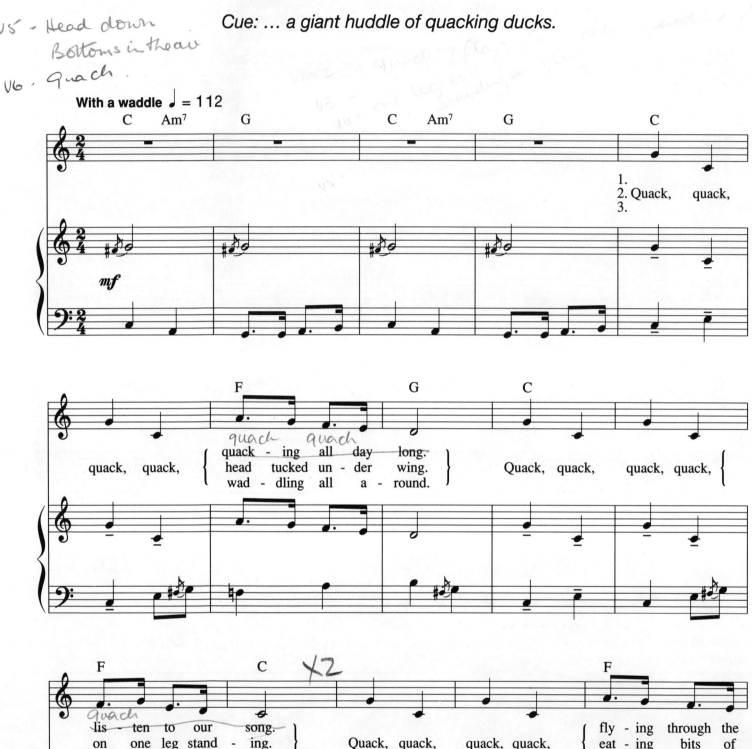

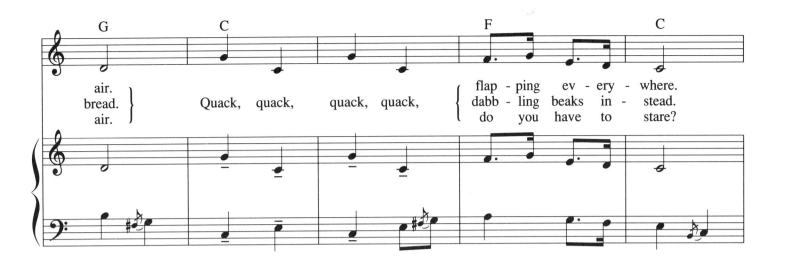

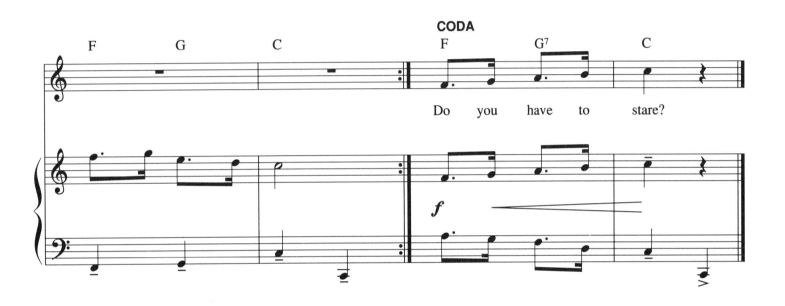

25

SONG 7
WE'VE FOUND YOU AT LAST

Repeat the song as necessary to perform a celebration dance.

Cue: The little lost kitten had been found at last!

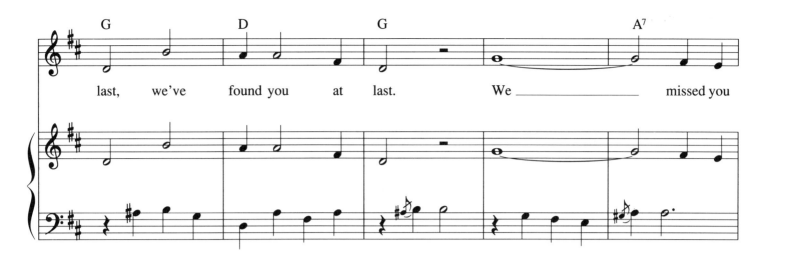

last, we've found you at last. We _____ missed you

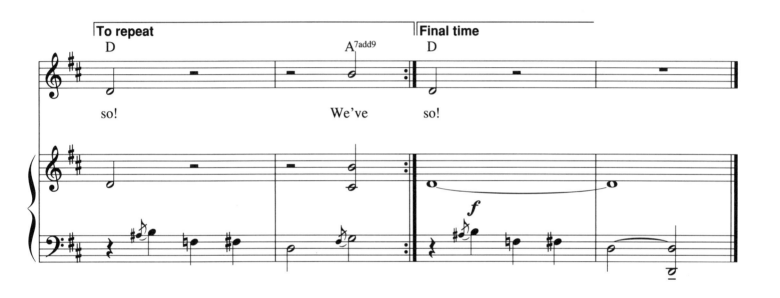

To repeat   **Final time**

so!   We've   so!

Page 28 is blank.

Printed and bound in Great Britain by
Caligraving Limited Thetford Norfolk